THE DATING JUNGLE

Adult Coloring Book

By Tara Richter

Published by Richter Publishing LLC www.richterpublishing.com

Editor: Marisa Beetz

Illustrations by Kate Tolpeeva and 123RF.com

ISBN: 978-1-945812-73-6 Paperback

DISCLAIMER

This book is designed to provide information on dating only. This information is provided and sold with the knowledge that the publisher and author do not offer any legal or medical advice. In the case of a need for any such expertise consult with the appropriate professional. This book does not contain all information available on the subject. This book has not been created to be specific to any individual people or organizations' situation or needs. Reasonable efforts have been made to make this book as accurate as possible. However, there may be typographical and or content errors. Therefore, this book should serve only as a general guide and not as the ultimate source of subject information. This book contains information that might be dated or erroneous and is intended only to educate and entertain. The author and publisher shall have no liability or responsibility to any person or entity regarding any loss or damage incurred, or alleged to have incurred, directly or indirectly, by the information contained in this book or as a result of anyone acting or failing to act upon the information in this book. You hereby agree never to sue and to hold the author and publisher harmless from any and all claims arising out of the information contained in this book. You hereby agree to be bound by this disclaimer, covenant not to sue and release. You may return this book within the guarantee time period for a full refund. In the interest of full disclosure, this book contains affiliate links that might pay the author or publisher a commission upon any purchase from the company. While the author and publisher take no responsibility for any virus or technical issues that could be caused by such kinks, the business practices of these companies and or the performance of any product or service, the author or publisher has used the product or service and makes a recommendation in good faith based on that experience. All characters appearing in this work are fictitious. Any resemblance to real persons, living or dead is purely coincidental.

DEDICATION

I dedicate this coloring book to all the hopeless romantics who have wasted too much time on dating apps, swiping left and right, hoping to find love. All those tragic first dates where the person showed up 20 years older and 200 pounds heavier than their profile photos.

Hopefully, this light-hearted coloring book will help you de-stress from your time spent in the dating jungle.

ACKNOWLEDGMENTS

I would like to thank Michael Murillo for giving me this million-dollar idea for a humorous dating coloring book that details the nuances of the modern dating world.

INTRODUCTION

Creating art has always been therapeutic for me. I have a degree in graphic design and used to have works of art juried into a gallery in downtown St. Petersburg, Florida. Along with painting and drawing, I love writing. This is even more healing, and it was so much fun to incorporate both of these into the fourth book in my *Dating Jungle* series. If you have been stuck in the dating jungle for a while, I hope these humorous adult dating tips allow you to relax and smile through the process. So pour yourself a glass of wine, get your colored pencils out, and have some fun! Post your finished pictures on social media with the hashtag #datingjunglecoloringbook and share with others in the jungle!

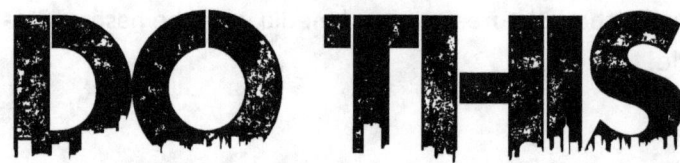

DO THIS

Meet up for a short coffee date first to see if you like each other. Make it short and sweet in the middle of the afternoon so there's not too much pressure on either side—especially if you are meeting up from a dating app. You want to make sure they actually look like the person they posted.

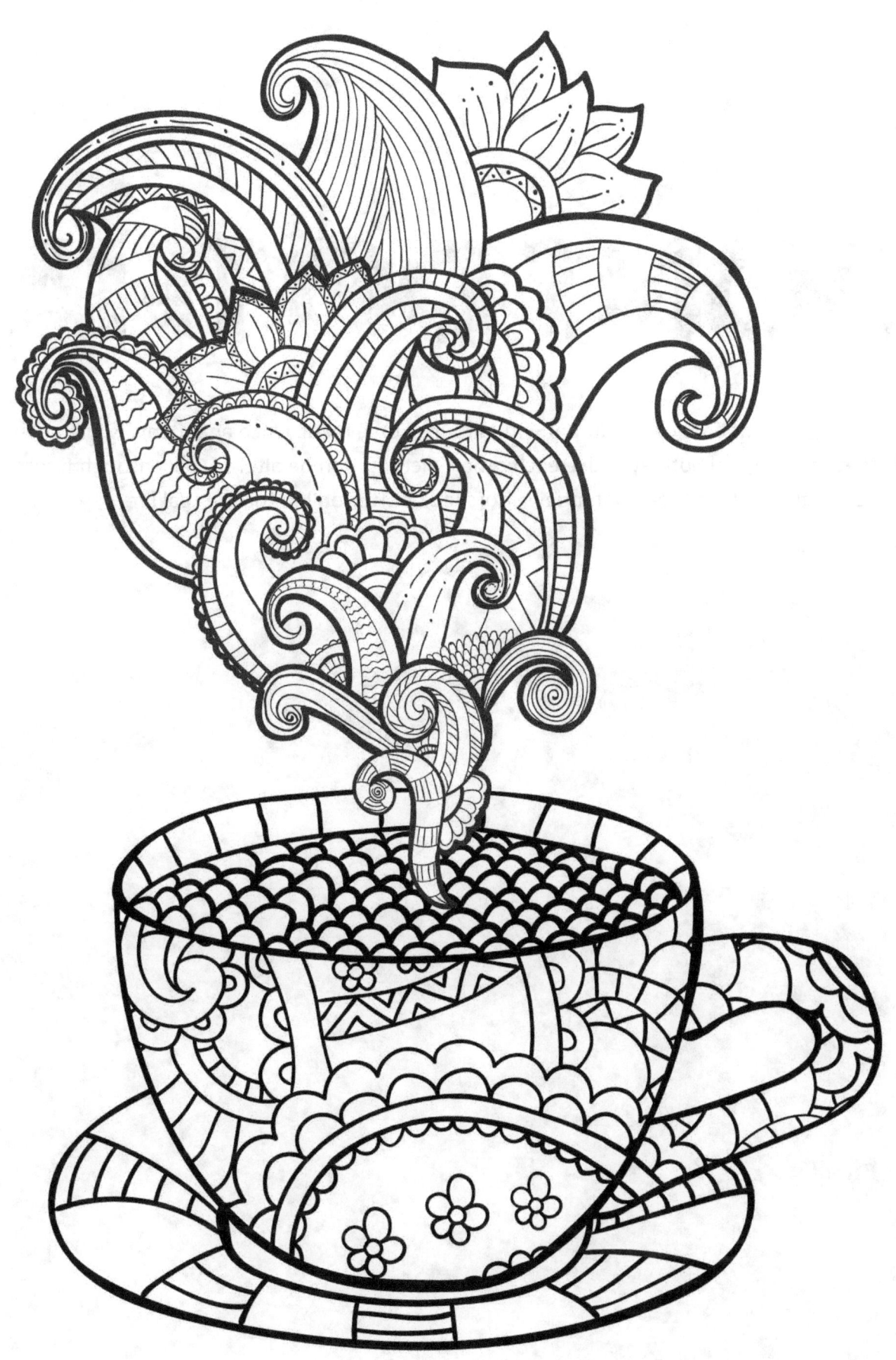

DON'T DO THAT

Go on a long date at a fancy restaurant with a four-course meal. Once again, this is just an initial meet and greet to see if you both even like each other. Pictures can be altered, put through filters, or taken at just the right angle to make potential suitors look better online than in real life.

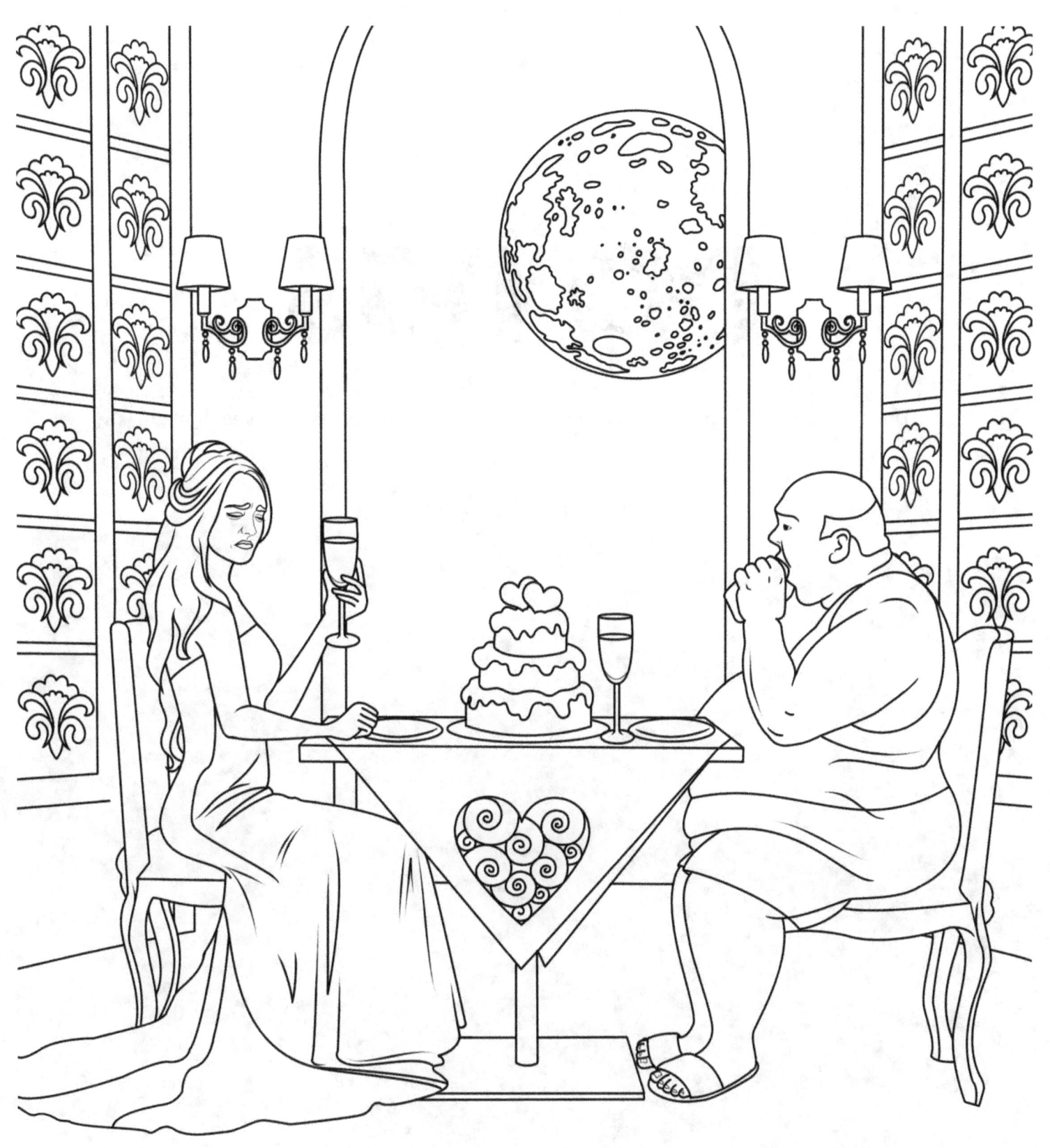

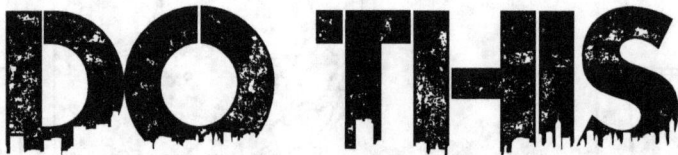

DO THIS

Dress up and look your best on first dates, but let your natural beauty shine through.

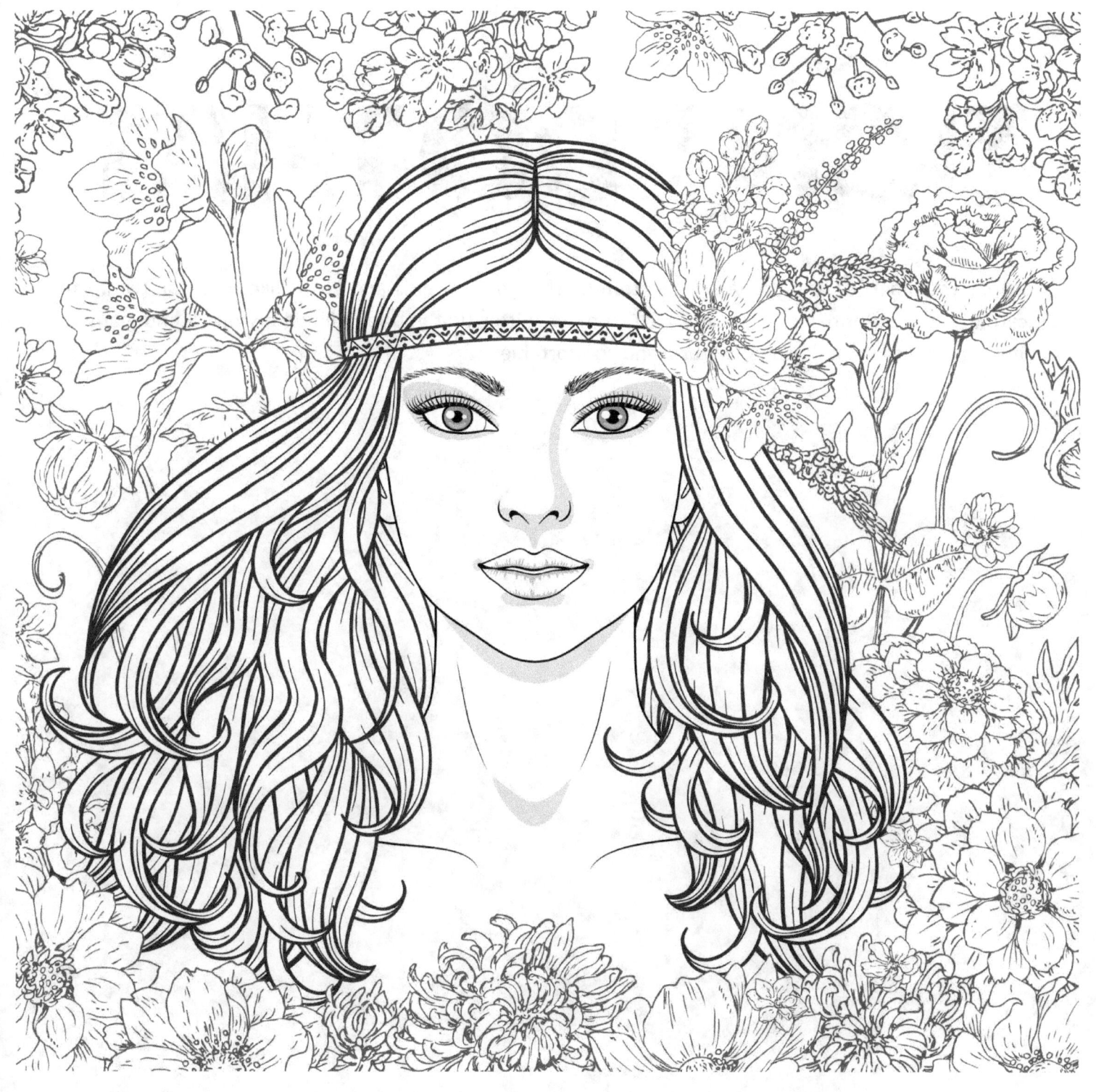

DONT DO THAT

Overdo your makeup and the latest hair trends. This goes for girls and guys alike. You don't want to scare off your potential love interest with so much glitter that you look like a disco ball and jeans so tight that you can't sit down. Be natural and comfortable.

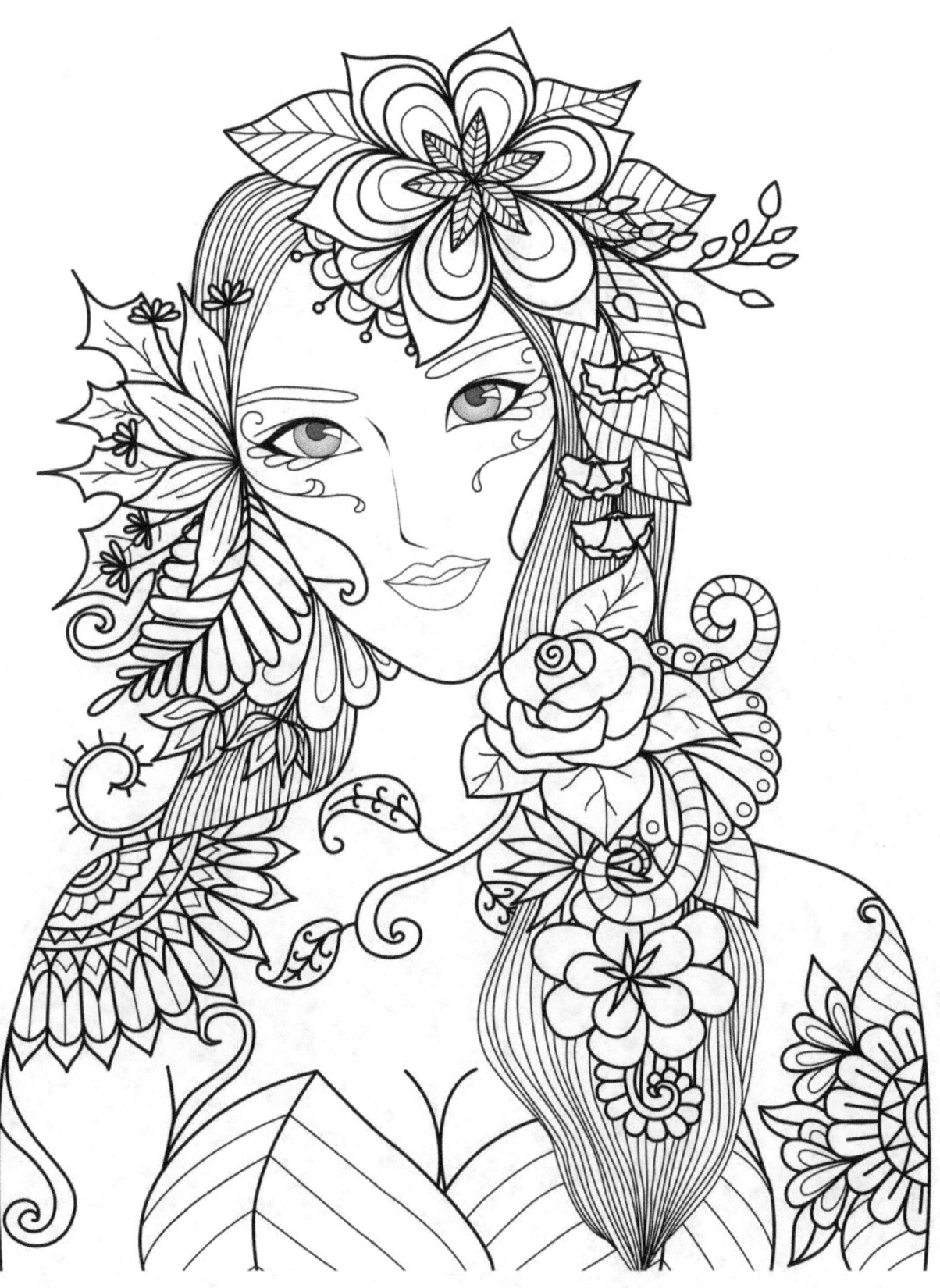

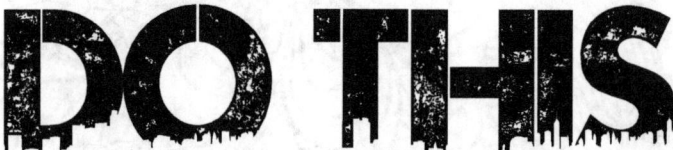

DO THIS

Talk about your pets and other hobbies you have. Think of fun topics and questions to ask the other person to keep them engaged. Light and fun conversations in the beginning are best.

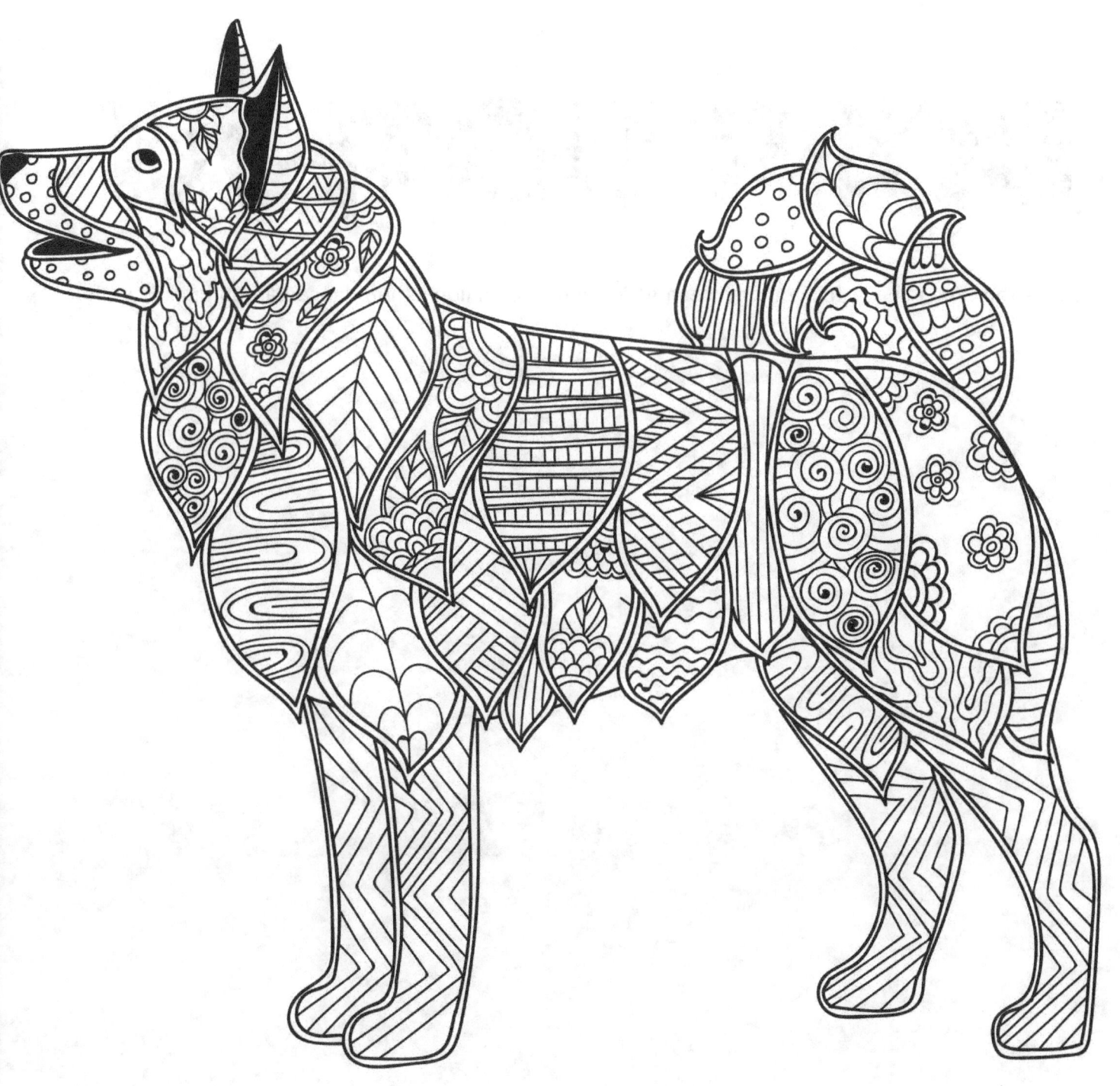

DON'T DO THAT

Discuss the time you got high on peyote in Africa and killed a lion—then danced around naked with it on your head.

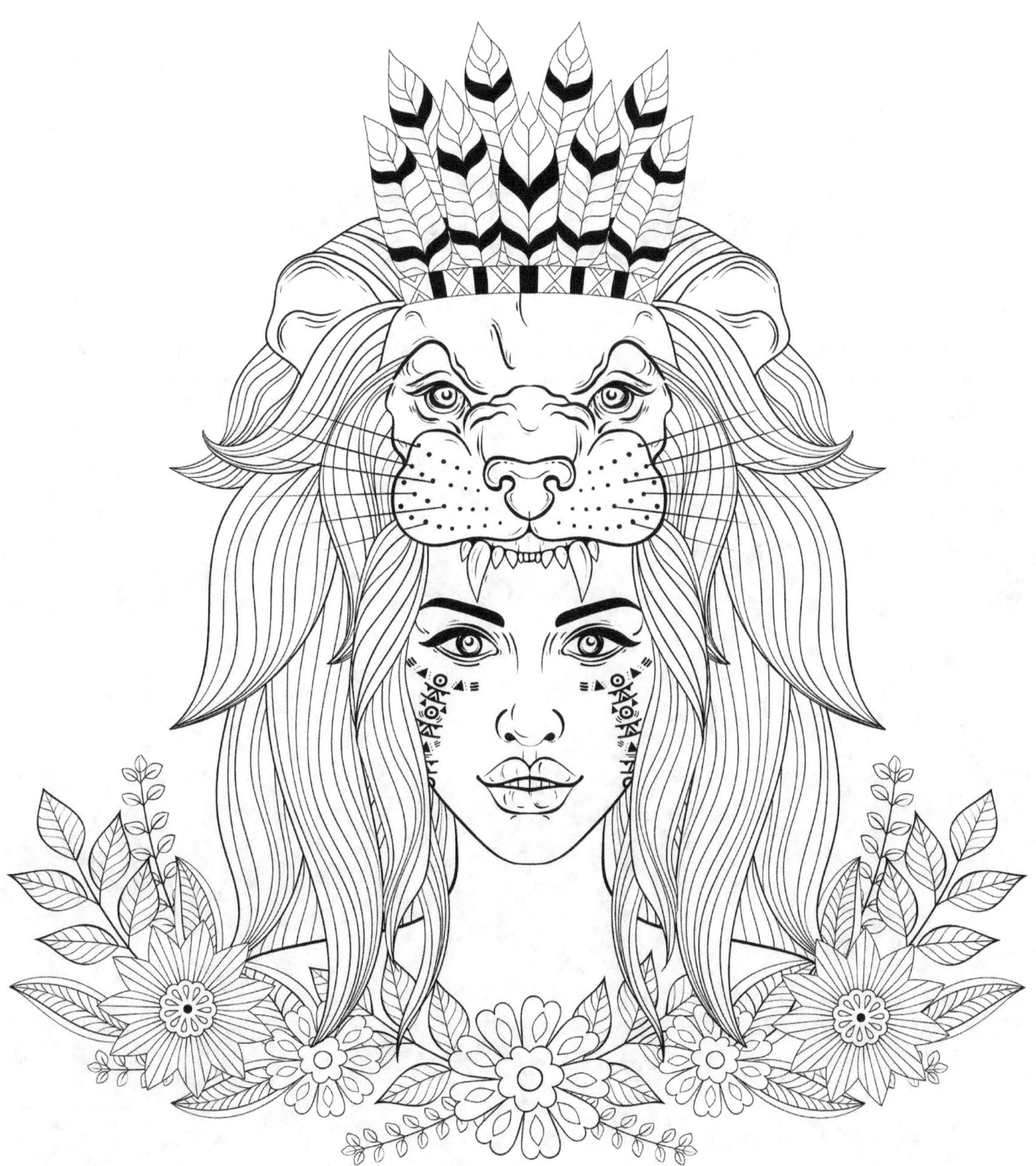

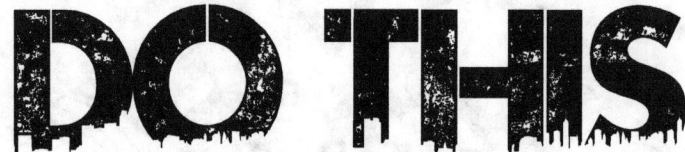

DO THIS

Exchange phone numbers, so you can chat before the date and also be in communication in case you get lost trying to find the place. Don't worry if they end up being a psycho—most phones have a blocking feature.

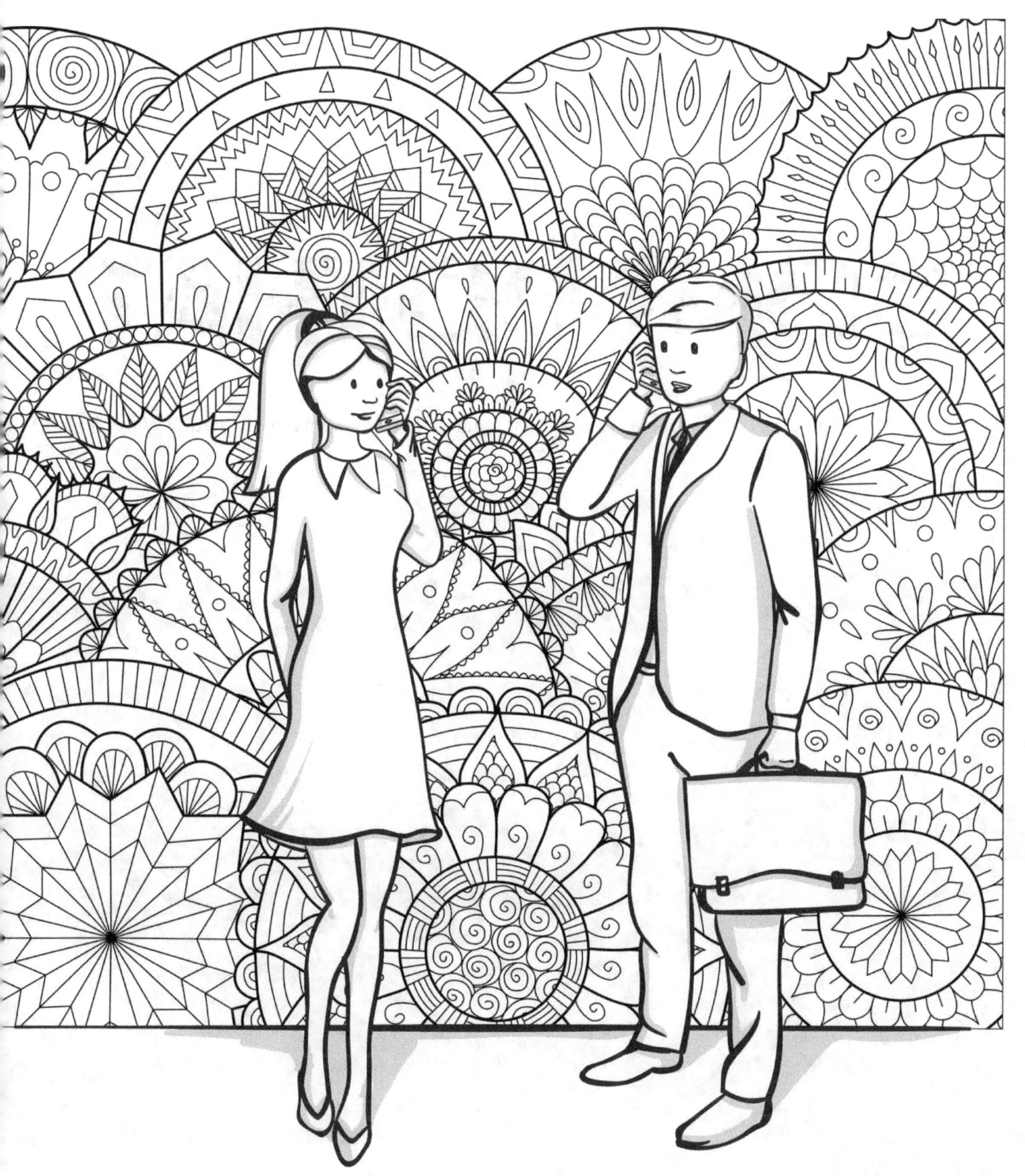

DON'T DO THAT

Send a dick pic as soon as you get their number. Nobody wants to see that.

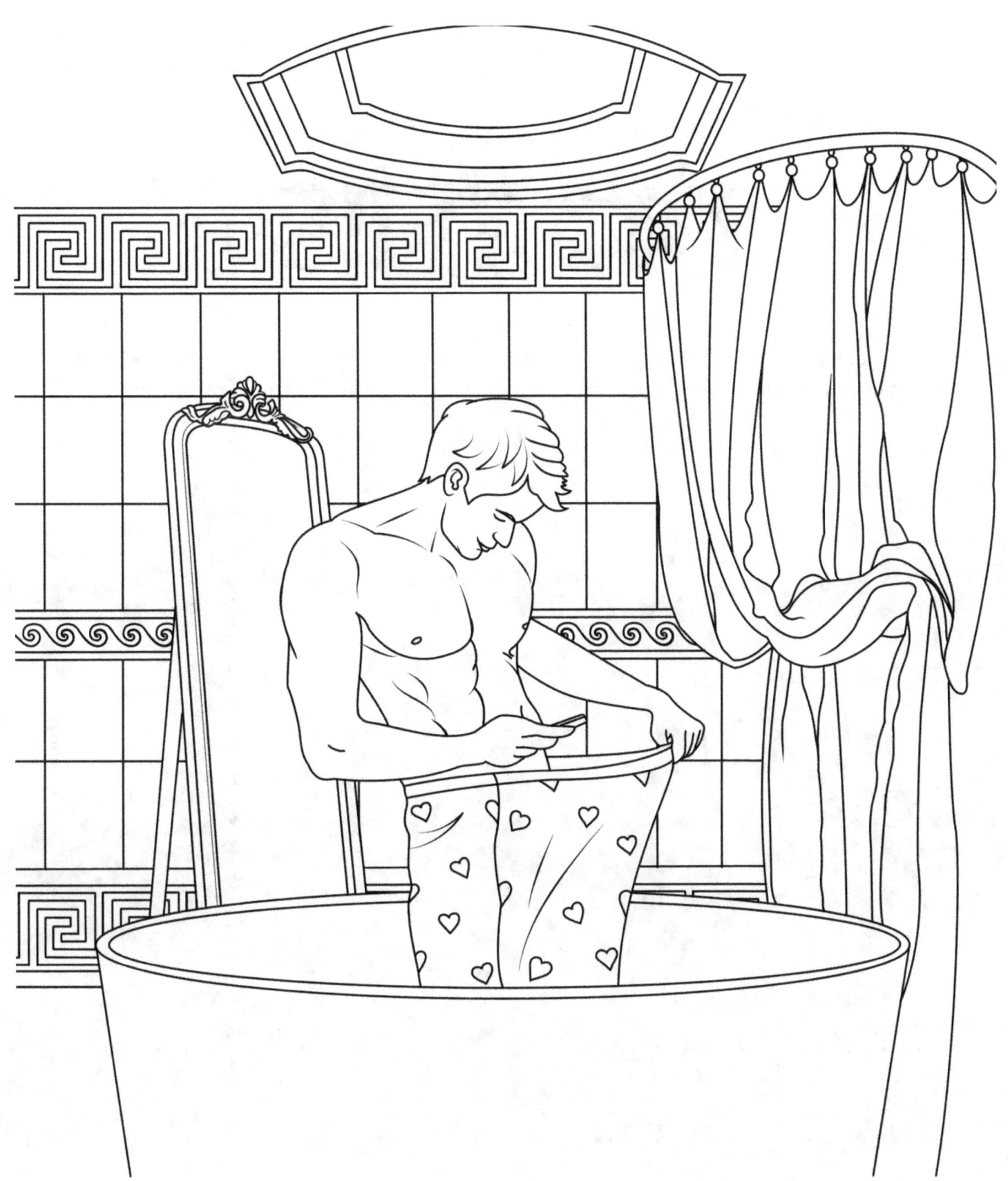

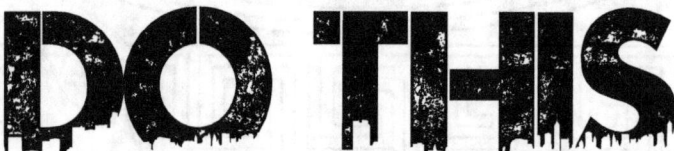

DO THIS

Show up with flowers and do other sweet gestures. An example would be finding out how they take their coffee, so you can surprise them by ordering it on their behalf the next time you see them.

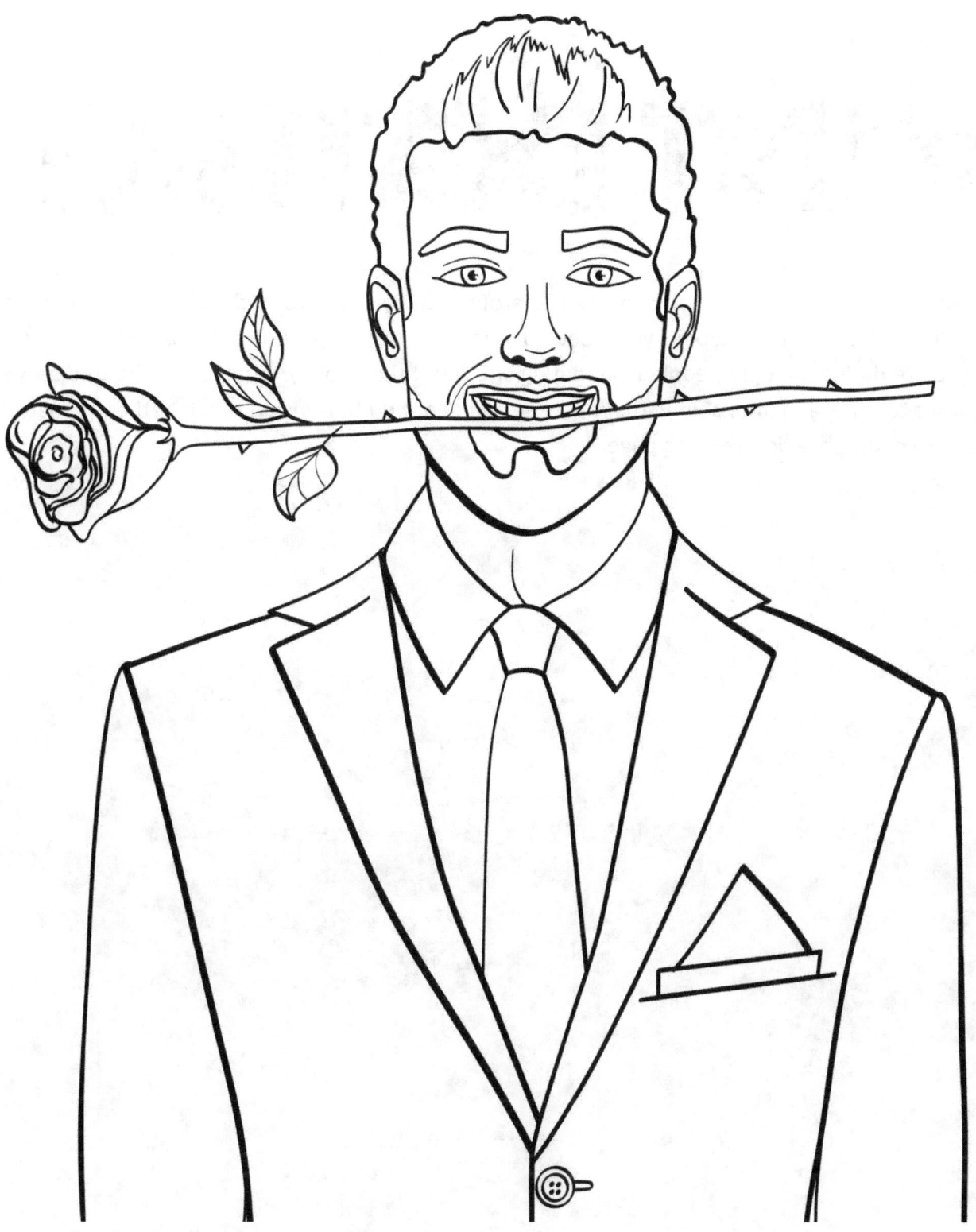

DON'T DO THAT

Stalk the girl you are interested in and follow her around everywhere to find out what she's up to. When you first start dating someone, you need to give each other space. Don't assume exclusivity. Most people are dating multiple people from dating sites, and that's okay. It takes a while to discover who you want to have a relationship with. You need to have the relationship talk together as mature adults, so both people are on the same page.

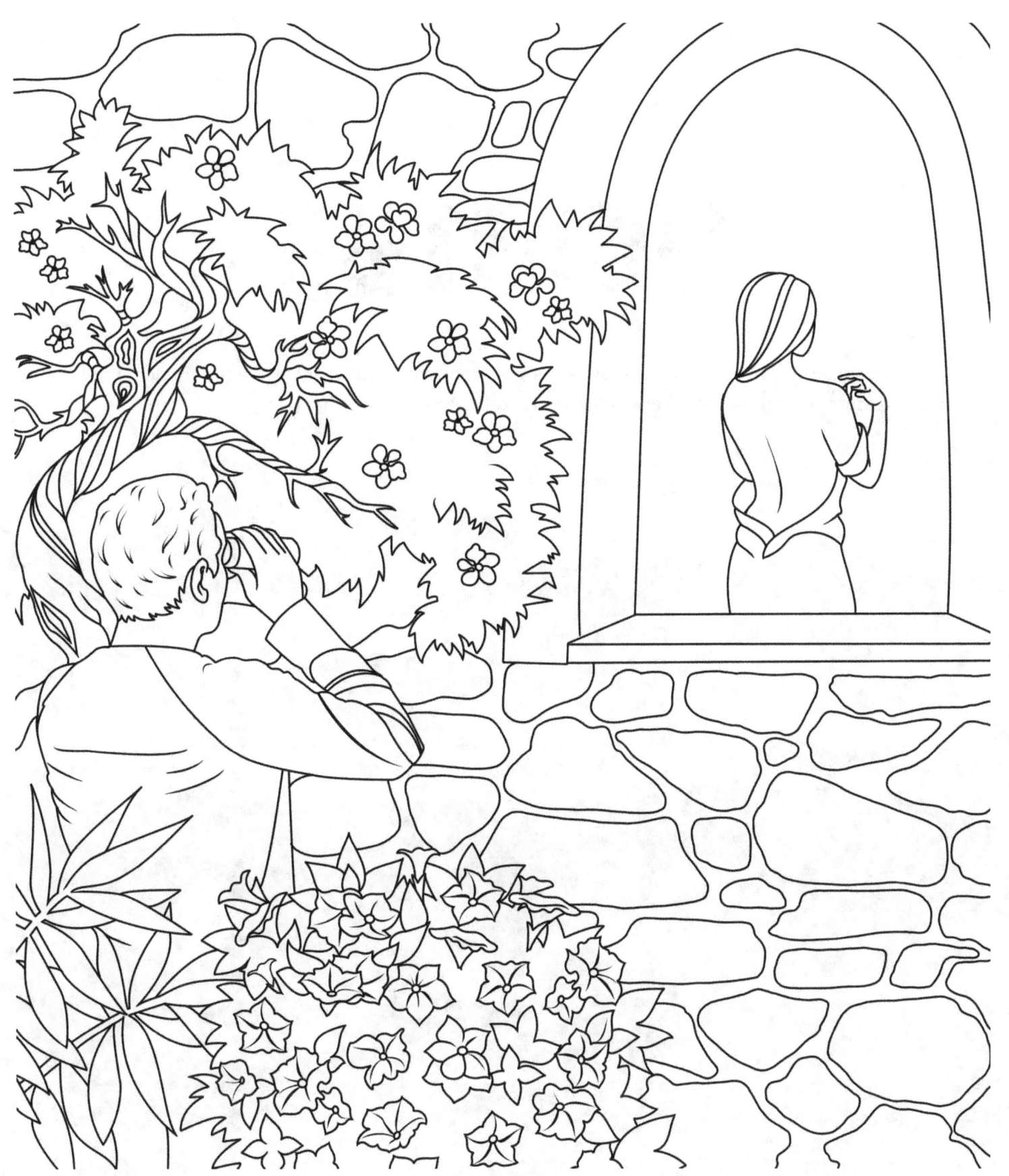

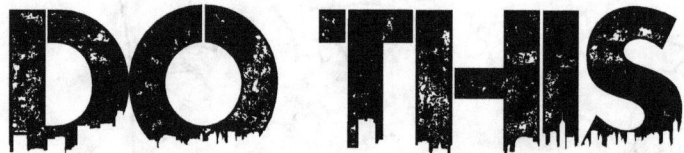

DO THIS

Go out for drinks and have fun. Remember, dating is supposed to be an enjoyable experience. Too much pressure ruins the atmosphere. A few drinks can take the edge off.

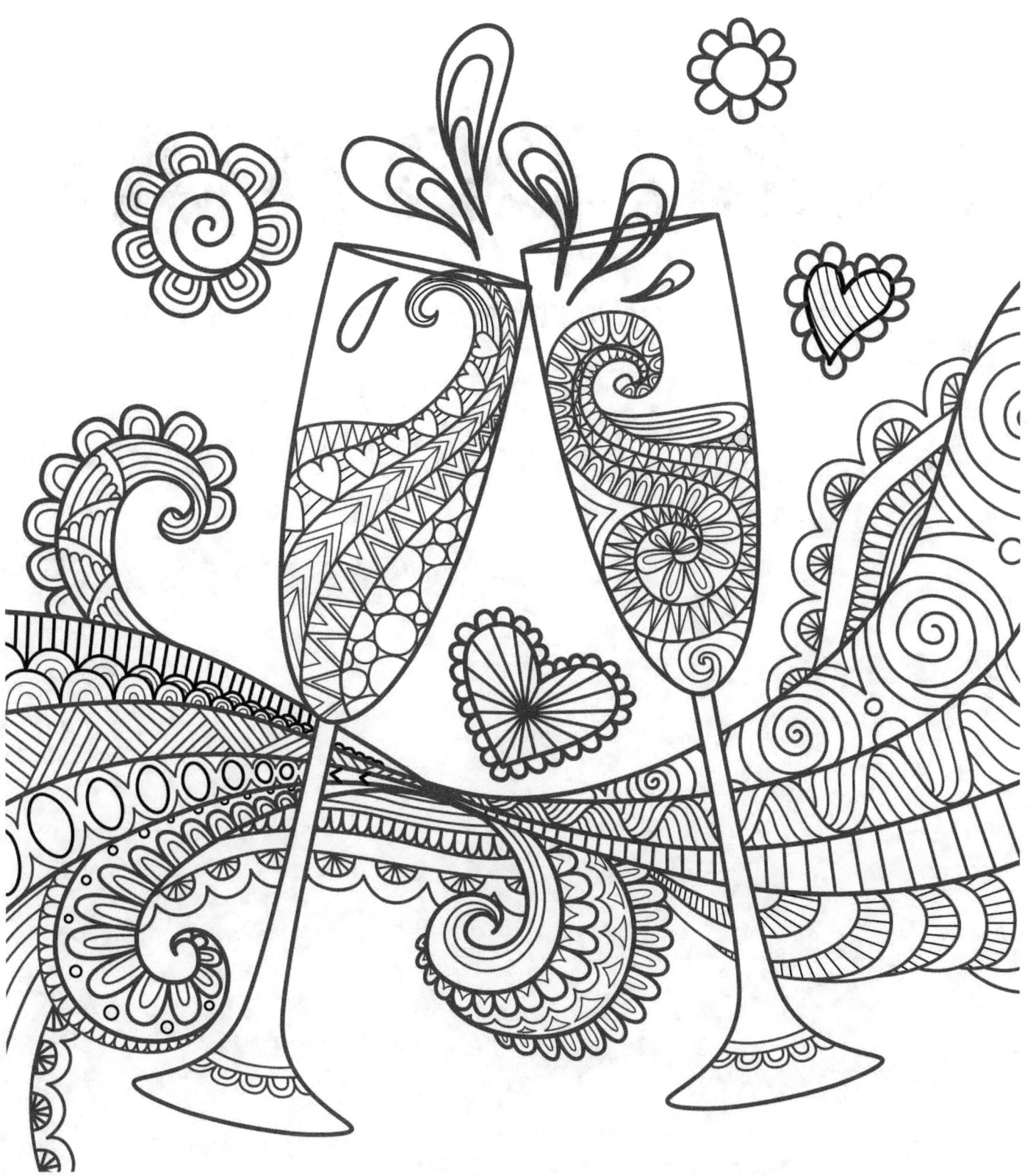

DON'T DO THAT

Drink too much and get wasted, dance on the tables, make out with the waiter, and flash the restaurant.

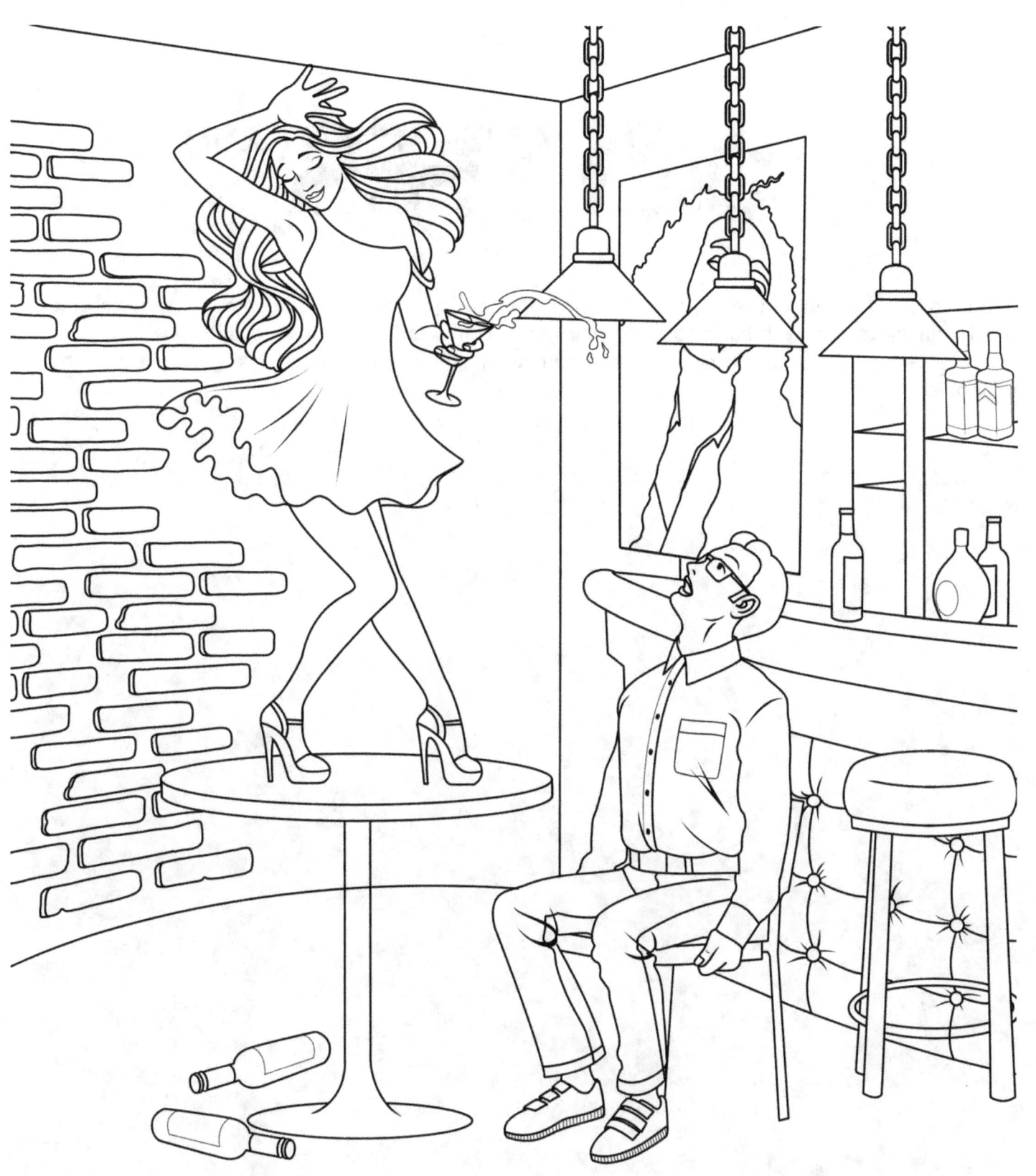

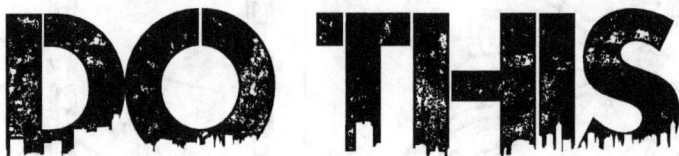

DO THIS

Relax and take time out for yourself during the dating process. Sometimes it can become overwhelming to deal with bad dates, too many stale conversations, and weeding through a million messages a day. Remember being single is not a negative thing—you are just taking time to find the right person for you.

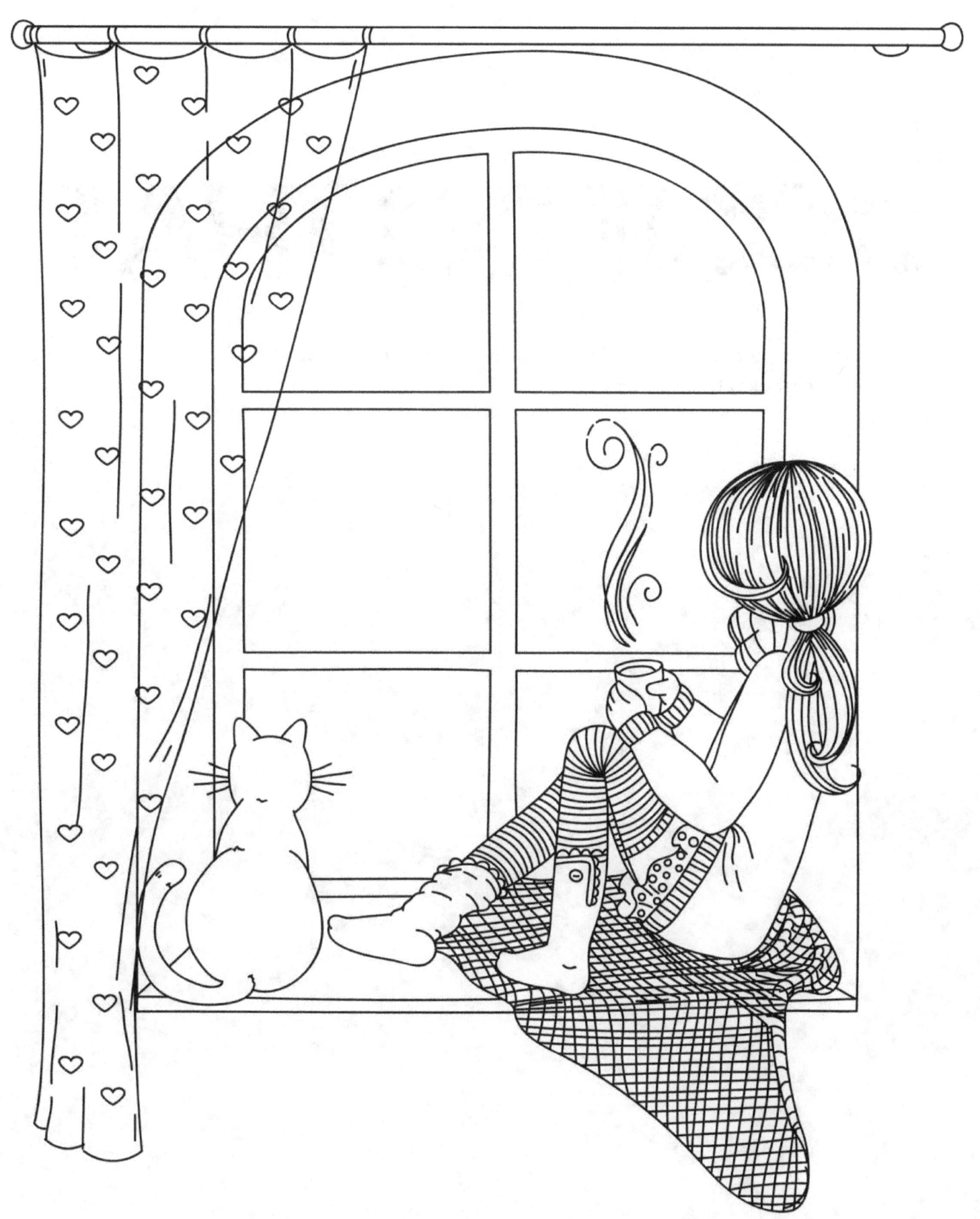

DON'T DO THAT

Once you have gone out on a few dates with the same person, now it's okay to send a dick pic. WRONG! It's never okay to send a dick pic.

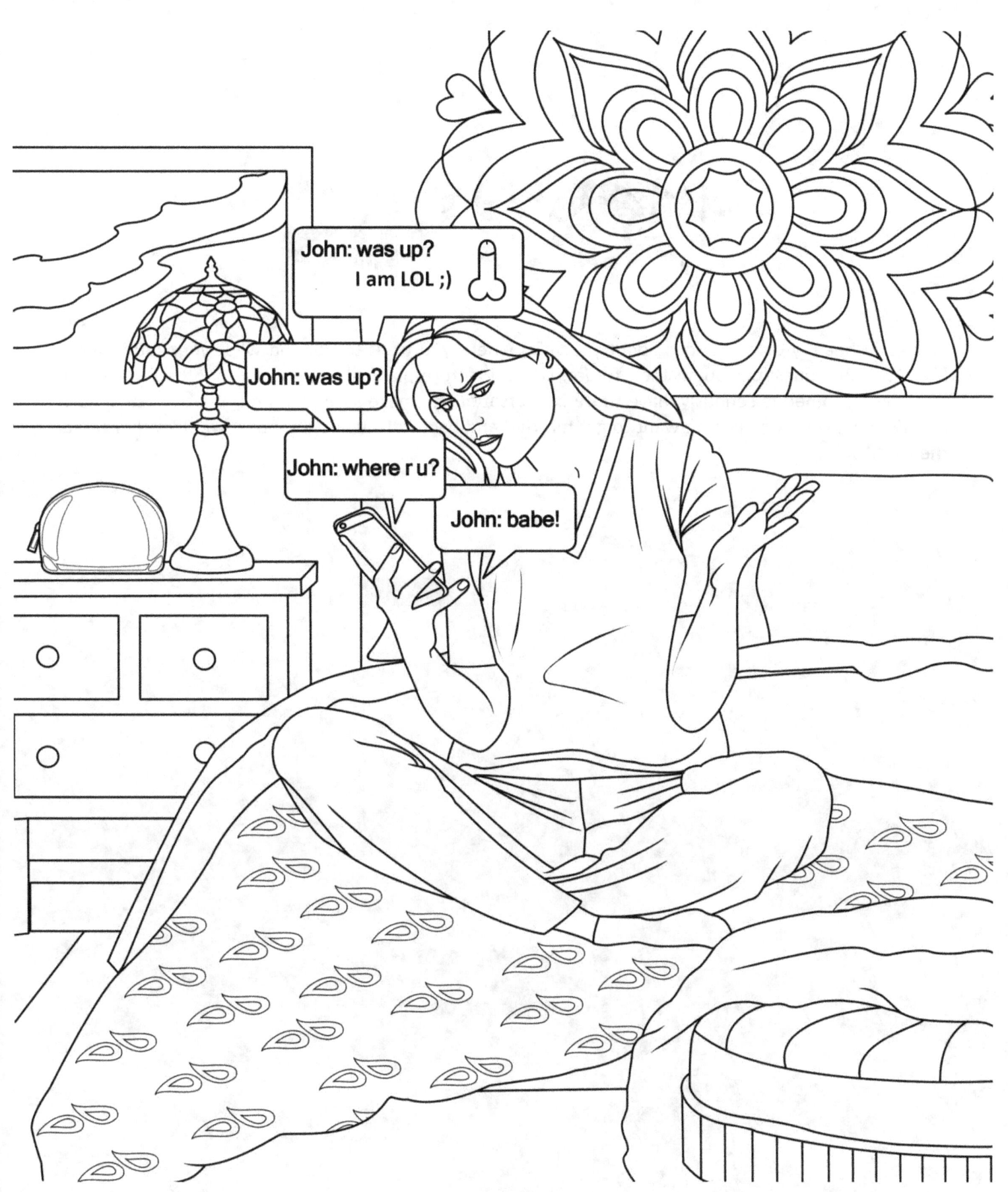

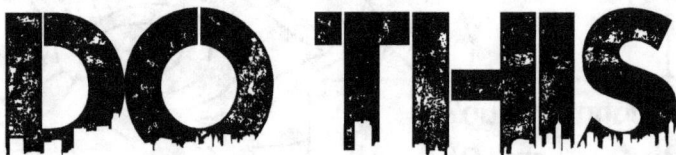

DO THIS

Engage in healthy conversations about your life, where you want to be, and what your future looks like. Ask them questions about their future. Do your future plans align with one another? Once you start dating someone seriously, have those conversations to make sure you are not just wasting each other's time. Does one person want to get married and have kids, while the other would rather travel the world solo?

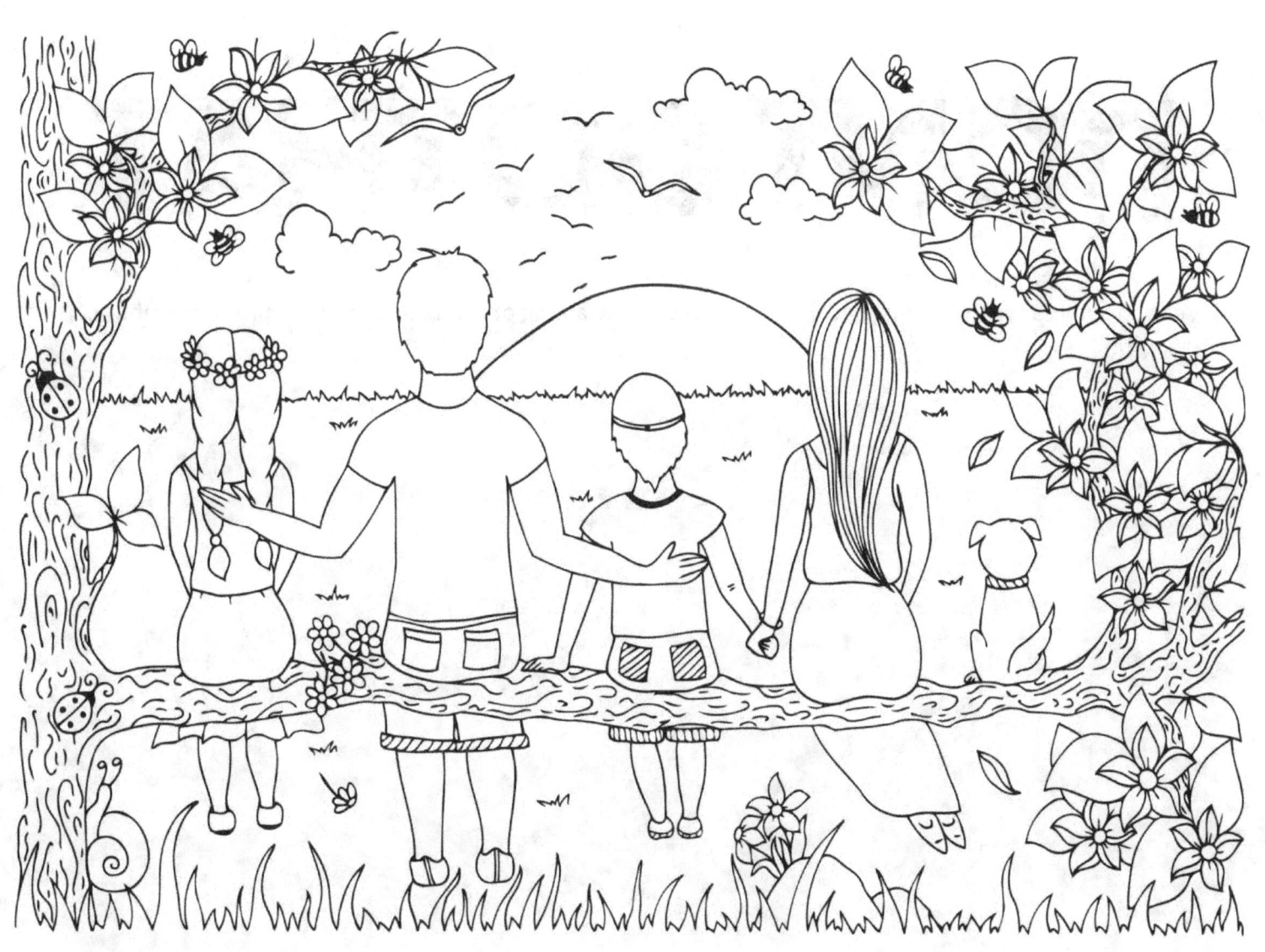

DON'T DO THAT

Vent about your crazy ex-husband who you have a restraining order against and is a proud member of the NRA.

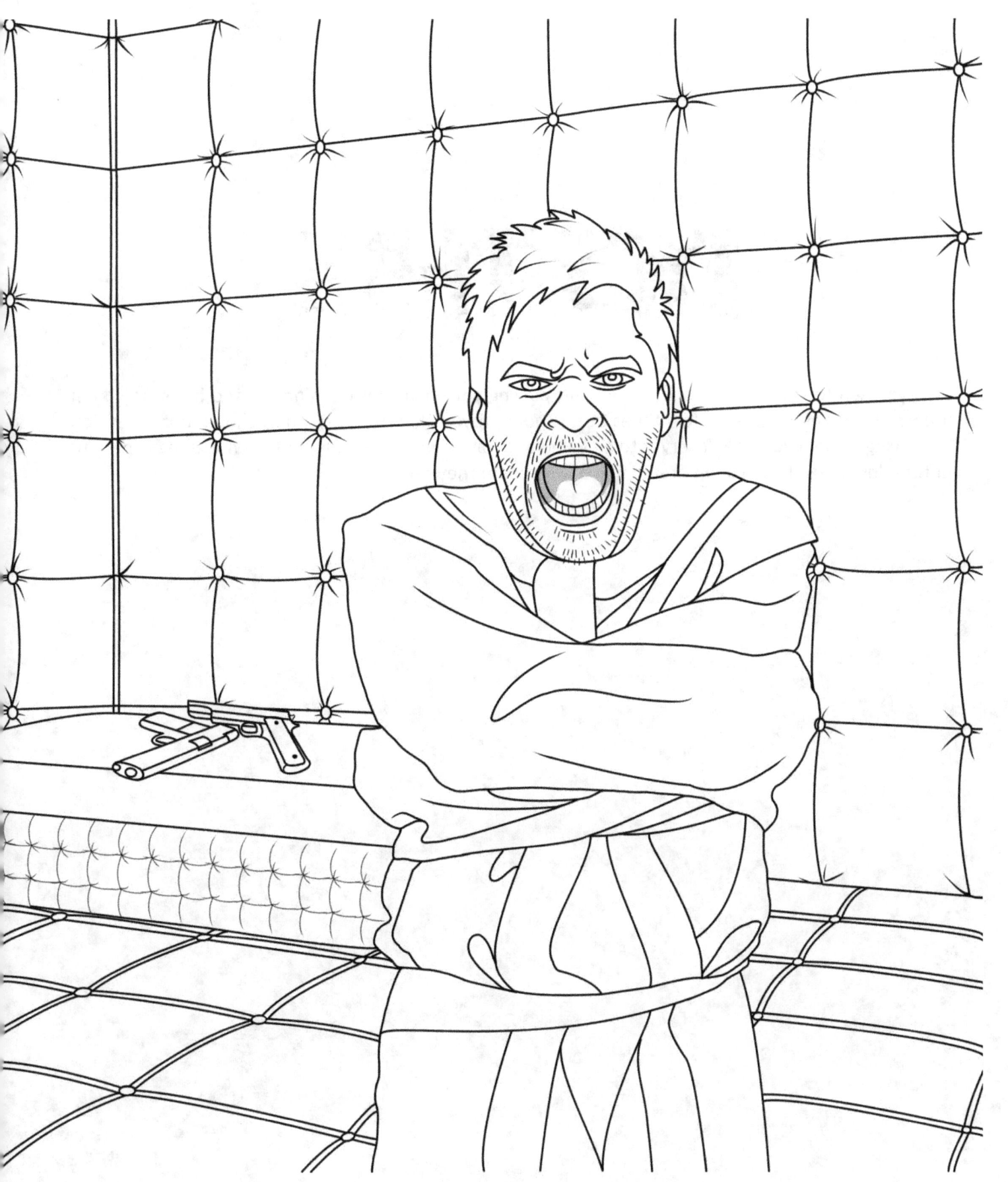

35

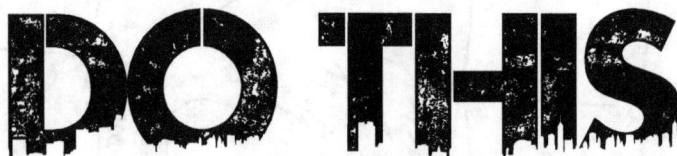

DO THIS

Allow yourself to fall in love again. It's difficult putting your heart in the hands of another person. I'm sure you have been burned a few times at this point in your life. However, that should not deter you from trying again. Everyone deserves to be loved and have love in their life, but it's not an easy path to venture down. Just take a deep breath and enjoy the journey.

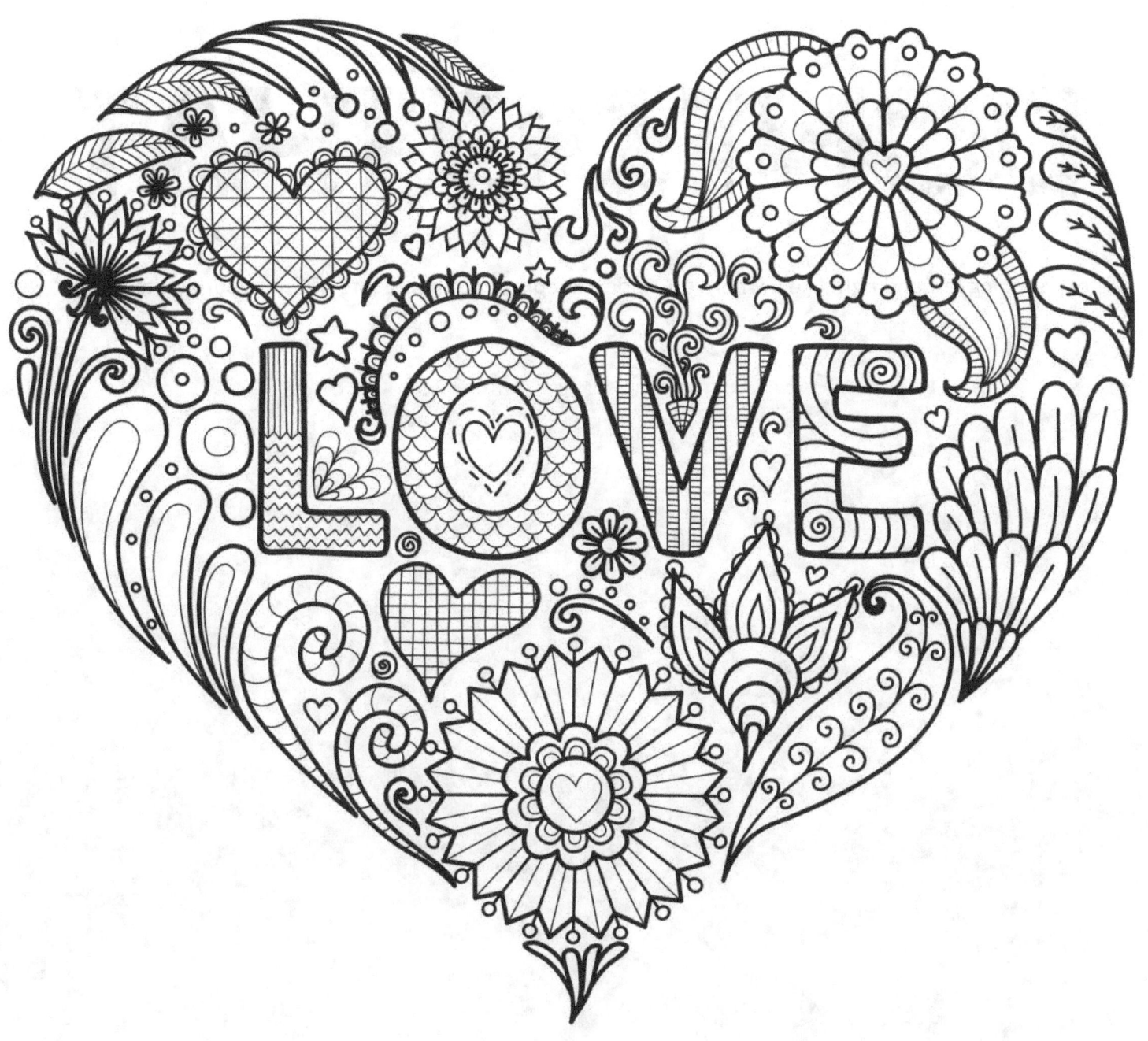

DON'T DO THAT

Keep swiping left and right like a whore on Tinder, keeping your heart safe but not your genitals.

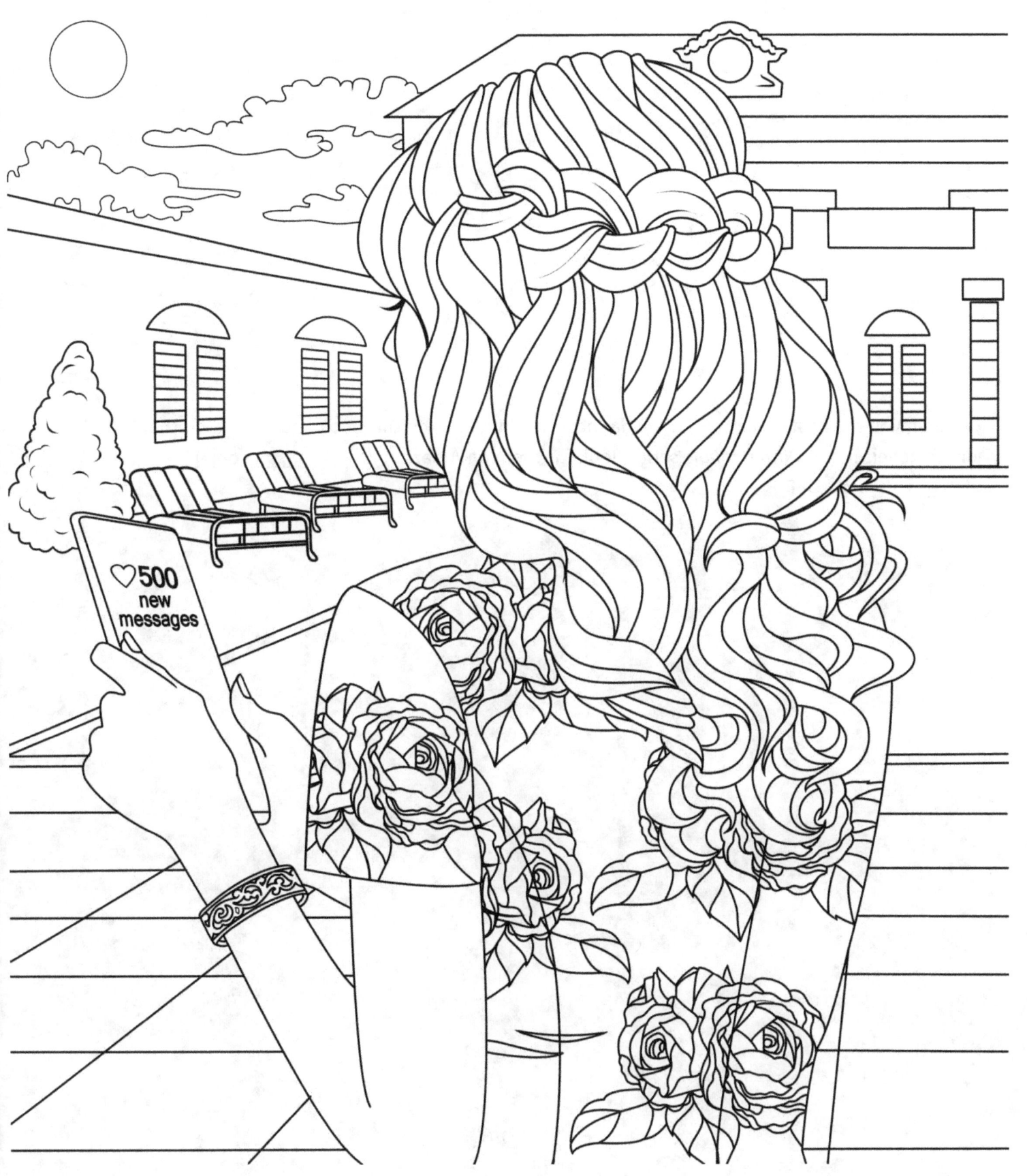

500
new
messages

We wish you the best of luck out in the dating jungle! If you liked this book and want the other full-length novels in the *Dating Jungle* series, look for them on Amazon: www.amazon.com/Tara-Richter/e/B00CGKD8FG

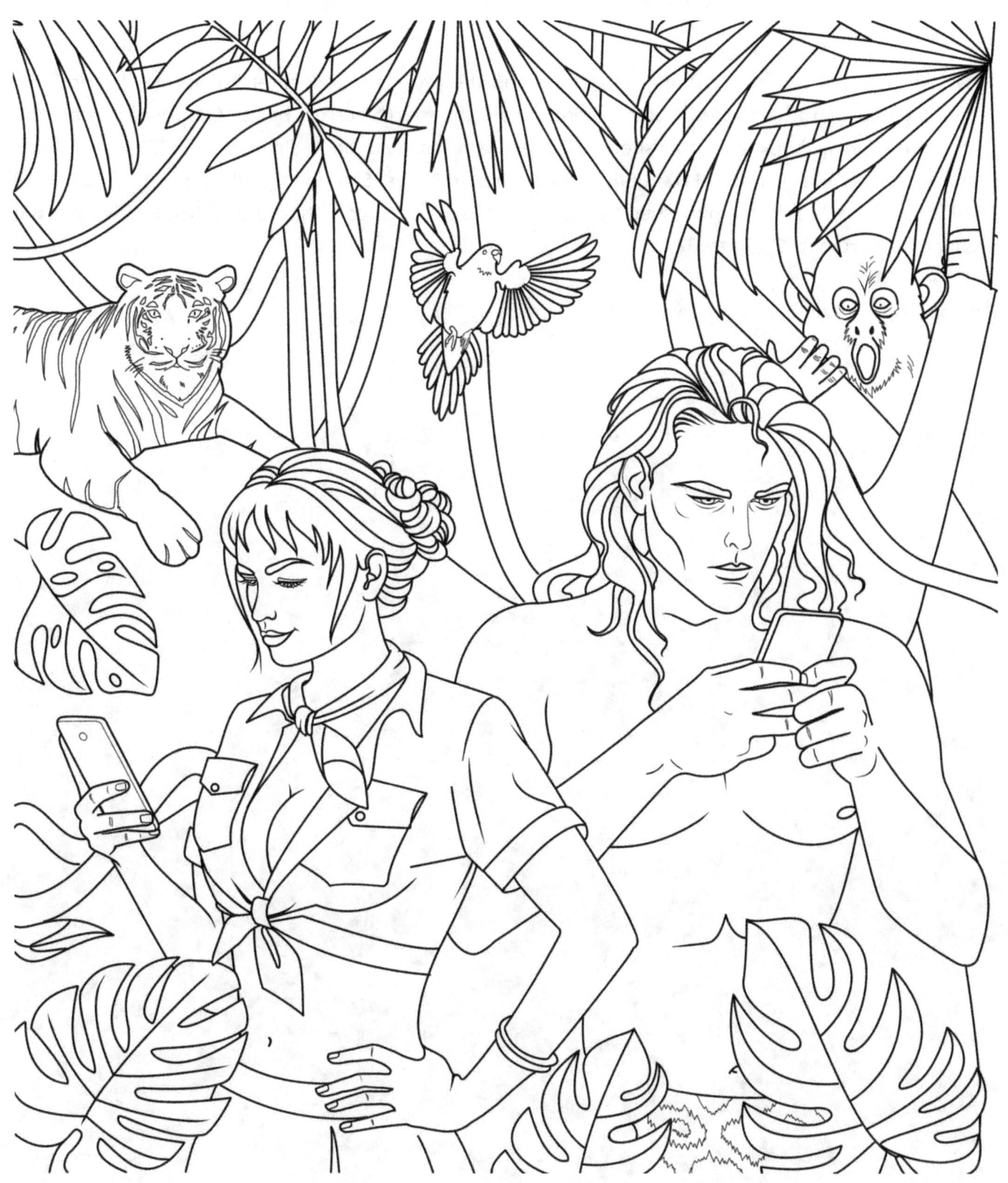

ABOUT THE AUTHOR

Tara Richter is the author of 10 different books and the president of Richter Publishing LLC, an indie publishing house located in Clearwater, Florida. This is the fourth book in her *Dating Jungle* series. The first *Dating Jungle* book was published in 2010. Tara has held book signings with CNN and been featured on Daytime TV, ABC, FOX, BBC, and Channel 10 News. She opened Richter Publishing LLC in 2014. One of the first books published by Richter Publishing was coauthored by Kevin Harrington, the original shark from ABC's *Shark Tank*.

Find out more about Tara on her website: www.richterpublishing.com

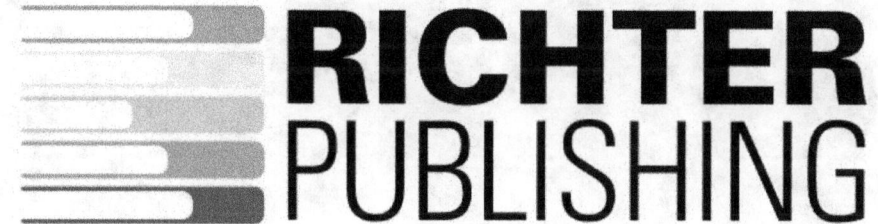